IMAGES
of Scotland

LIVINGSTON

IMAGES
of Scotland

LIVINGSTON

Compiled by
William F. Hendrie

TEMPUS

First published 2000
Copyright © William F. Hendrie, 2000

Tempus Publishing Limited
The Mill, Brimscombe Port,
Stroud, Gloucestershire, GL5 2QG

ISBN 0 7524 1888 2

Typesetting and origination by
Tempus Publishing Limited
Printed in Great Britain by
Midway Clark Printing, Wiltshire

Contents

Acknowledgements

My thanks to Dr Arthur Down, Rae Rutherford, Linda Wood, Alison McCormack, the staff of the former Livigston Development Corporation, Martin Boyle and Lindsay Gould of the *West Lothian Courier* for help with providing pictures and information for this book.

Introduction

Livingston is West Lothian's largest town and indeed, apart from Scotland's capital city, Edinburgh, by far the largest place in the whole of the Lothians. During the past forty years over 40,000 people have chosen to make it their home, which is a remarkable achievement considering that before the 1960s few beyond its immediate area had ever even heard of it. All that changed in 1962 when the Government was seeking a suitable place to relocate Glasgow's surplus population and chose this beautiful area on the banks of the River Almond in the lea of the Pentland Hills to the south and the Bathgate Hills to the north, midway between Glasgow and Edinburgh, to be the attractive site for the fourth of Scotland's five designated New Towns.

The post-Second World War planners were, however, not the first to recognize the benefits which Livingston offered as a place to live. Way back in the eleventh century, about the same time as the Battle of Hastings in England, Scotland's kings chose this sheltered valley as the site for one of their royal hunting lodges.

In those historic times the lands around Livingston were amongst the richest in Scotland in their abundance of game, from large red deer to small but extremely ferocious wild boar. Later, during what became known as the peaceful Norman Conquest of Scotland in the twelfth century, King Alexander invited a Flemish nobleman called De Leving to settle and develop an estate in this area. To secure his acquisition, De Leving constructed a tall square thick stone walled keep or peel tower. Soon cottages grew up around it to provide homes for the servants needed to run it. These houses first bore the name Leving's Toun from which the present Livingston is derived. De Leving did well in the country of his adoption and his heirs became famous as the Livingstons, who became hereditary keepers of Linlithgow Palace and gained the title of Lord Linlithgow. Livingston Peel was occupied by a branch of the family until in the sixteenth century they failed to produce an heir and the estate was acquired by the Murrays of Elibank, who were a well known Borders' family. Best known of the Murrays of Livingston was Baron Patrick. He was one of Scotland's earliest botanists and created a beautiful garden round the foot of the Peel. It included orchards and a spectacular Italian-style water garden complete with fountains, pools and waterfalls. He was so enthusiastic that he decided to travel to the Continent to gather new specimens for his garden at Livingston. He wrote home describing the many new plants which he had discovered. Sadly, he did not live to see them planted as while staying at Avignon, in the south of France, he caught a chill which developed into a fever, culminating in his death in

1671. Back in Scotland, his friends, who included the King's physician and West Lothian's earliest historian, Sir Robert Sibbald, saved his collection and transferred it to Edinburgh, where the plants and flowers formed the nucleus from which the city's famous Royal Botanic Gardens grew. Even after Baron Murray's untimely death, his heirs continued to take a great interest in the development of the Livingston estate and in the eighteenth century introduced all the latest agricultural developments, including the planting of shelter belts of deciduous trees, some of which still survive among the one million planted by Livingston Development Corporation in more modern times.

Links with Livingston's rich agricultural past are preserved at the Almond Valley Heritage Centre, which incorporates Livingston Mill and Farm. The Heritage Centre is also the official museum of the Scottish shale-oil industry, whose development in Victorian times so transformed the Livingston area. The great changes that took place in the nineteenth century were, however, nothing compared to the vast developments which have taken place in the last four decades of the twentieth century, when Livingston's classification as one of Scotland's five official New Towns resulted in such dramatic growth that it is now the administrative, economic and shopping centre for the whole of West Lothian.

One

Village Life

Historic Livingston Village is today a tranquil haven in the heart of the bustle of life in the flourishing modern town, with its picturesque eighteenth-century church, its former coaching inn and its rows of traditional old stone-built slate-roofed cottage homes, a delightful reminder of what life was like in years gone by. The present kirk building dates from when it was built in 1732 in typical plain unadorned Scottish Presbyterian style, but it is known that worship on this site took place from earlier times. There are written mentions of a chapel in the fourteenth century, where the monks from Holyrood Abbey in Edinburgh celebrated Mass. After the Reformation in 1560 it became the district's first place of Protestant worship and services were held regularly until 1650, when the troops of the Lord High Protector, Oliver Cromwell, destroyed the building at the start of the Commonwealth period.

Two centuries later Livingston Kirk faced another threat to its peaceful existence in the form of the dreaded resurrectionists, the much feared corpse vandals, who preyed on Lothian's churchyards as conveniently situated sources of fresh bodies, to supply the need of Professor Knox for corpses for his students at the medical school of Edinburgh University to practise their dissection on. To try to thwart the body-snatchers, as they were commonly known, the minister, the Revd James M. Robertson, petitioned local landowner, Lord Hopetoun, to purchase six heavy iron lattice-work covers called mortsafes, to place over all new graves for three weeks until the bodies in them had deteriorated sufficiently to be of no value. His lordship agreed and shortly afterwards the mortsafes were ordered from the Shotts Ironworks in neighbouring Lanarkshire and purchased at a cost of five guineas each. The threat to Livingston of raids by the body-snatchers came about because of the existence of the southern toll road between Edinburgh and Glasgow , which was constructed through the district in 1756 and which made Livingston much more accessible. The Old Toll House on the road to Whitburn is a reminder of this development and the use of this route by stage coaches also gave rise to the construction of the inn in the centre of the village, which became a regular stopping place on the long twelve-hour journey between the two cities. While the teams of horses which pulled the mail-coaches were changed or watered, the passengers enjoyed refreshments at the inn, which is still a popular hostelry to this day for both locals and visitors alike.

Built in true Presbyterian style in 1732, Livingston Kirk's only external adornment is its simple rooftop lantern belfry. Despite its lack of decoration, however, this severely simple place of worship has several interesting features. It was specifically designed with its pulpit in the middle of the long north wall so that the minister could be at the heart of his congregation and so that its members could gather as closely as possible around the holy table in front of it to share in communion. According to the Second Statistical Account of Scotland, published in 1843, the church had a congregation of 636, consisting of 314 men and 322 women, and had a seating capacity of 300. There was, however, apparently no problem with overcrowding as it was difficult for many members of the congregation to attend, because of the remote and scattered nature of the parish. The minister who wrote the report, the Revd James M. Robertson, who concluded his forty years of service to the parish in the year of its publication, stated that 'the church is very inconveniently situated for at least three-fourths of the population. The number regularly attending is too fluctuating to be exactly ascertained.'

In earlier centuries church discipline was much stricter than today and an example of how it was imposed on any erring members of the Livingston congregation can still be seen next to the entrance in the form of the finger pillory, where miscreants who had offended the Kirk Session, the court of the church, were punished by having to stand in this prominent position in full view of their fellow worshippers for the entire length of the service, which often went on for two or more hours. Unlike today, members of the congregation had to pay for the privilege of attending church, through seat rents, which had to be paid four times every year. It was only after their quarterly seat rent had been duly paid that worshippers had the right to 'sneck the yett', that is to close the door on their timber box pews.

Charges of another kind were imposed at the Old Toll House at Long Livingston, just to the west of Livingston Village on the main road from Livingston to Whitburn, where all vehicles using the southern route between Edinburgh and Glasgow via Whitburn had to stop to pay tolls. Of symmetrical Georgian design, it was erected in 1756 and still stands on the south side of the road.

Unlike the Old Toll House at Long Livingston, Howden Toll House, shown in this very early photograph, has sadly not survived. Originally, as well as collecting fees from passing road users, the toll houses used to sell spirits and ales to travellers on their long and often cold journeys. The toll houses were therefore Livingston's original licensed premises, but later separate inns were opened. The one built close to the toll house in the previous picture, at Long Livingston, was known as the High House of Livingston and its very attractive landlady was immortalized in the old Scottish ballad, 'The Bonnie Lass o' Livingston'.

Opened in 1764, the twin stone-arched Howden Bridge across the waters of the River Almond was built to speed traffic on the new forty-four mile-long Southern Toll Road between Glasgow and Edinburgh.

Livingston Inn welcomed its first guests in 1764 when the new Toll Road brought stage coaches to the village for the first time. The new inn immediately became an established halt on the twelve-hour-long journey between the two Scottish cities and it is not difficult to conjure up the scene of hustle and bustle which the arrival of a coach must have created, as its passengers clambered down and clamoured to be served a warming drink and something to eat in the short time which it took to change the horses and speed it on its way again. In 1780 one of the coaches, which stopped daily at Livingston Inn, was advertised as 'The Edinburgh to Glasgow Flyer', but it still took it a full half day to complete the journey. Other coaches, including the one from Edinburgh to Kilmarnock, followed the other route through Livingston and Mid Calder and the old Elmtree Inn, in Bellsquarry, was a recognized stop on this journey.

The toll road originally snaked its way through the heart of Livingston Village and continued to do so until after the start of the New Town in 1962. Now, however, all traffic by-passes the old village, leaving it a much more peaceful and pleasant place to explore.

The construction of the Glasgow-to-Edinburgh railway line in 1840 soon robbed Livingston of its prosperous stagecoach passenger trade and the village became a quiet backwater again as this scene of rural tranquillity shows. This photograph of the deserted main road was taken during the early years of the 1900s. The only signs of activity were the two housewives chatting at the entrance to the old inn and the two wee lassies in their white 'pinnies' calling to each other from opposite sides of the empty road. It is interesting to note the absence of the large door in the wing of the inn jutting out into the road, shown in the picture at the foot of page twelve.

Much more extensive alterations were made to Livingston Inn after the start of the New Town in the 1960s, and this picture shows what it looked like at the end of the 1970s. (Photograph courtesy of John Doherty)

Fortunately the renovations of the 1960s and 1970s preserved some of the inn's former coaching day features, as can be seen in this attractive view of the old stable yard, where the stagecoaches used to stop two centuries before. (Photograph courtesy of John Doherty)

Livingston's historic kirk and the old inn are both seen at the far end of the village street in this picture taken towards the end of the 1970s. (Photograph courtesy of John Doherty)

Seen here delivering the morning 'pintas' to 'The Danders', the milk-boy used to be a regular daily visitor to homes in the village. Nowadays, like other New Town residents, householders in the village collect their supplies of milk from local supermarkets.

Perhaps the milk-boy was a pupil at Livingston Village School. Built shortly after the Scottish Education Act in 1872, the old school still stands in the village and is now used as a small centre for community activities. Built of stone and roofed with slate, it is a typically stern Victorian school whose no-nonsense architecture reflects the approach to education of a century ago. Its tall, narrow windows were set high in its classroom walls so that its pupils could not see out of them and thus be distracted from their study of the 'Three Rs,' 'Reading,' 'riting' and 'rithmetic'. The classrooms were heated by open coal fires, whose tall chimneys can still be seen, and the teacher's high wooden desk and chair were placed next to the hearth where they could keep cosily warm, while their pupils froze. There was no nonsense about children's 'rights' and chilled fingers were a reminder of their responsibility to keep on working diligently, or be warmed with the stinging, searing strokes of the strap, whose twin or triple leather thongs bit like a snake. The playground was surrounded by a solid stone wall with iron gates.

The old Schoolhouse, the substantial stone-built home of the dominie, is seen from the rear in this picture taken in the opposite direction to the one in which the milk-boy is seen making his delivery on the previous page. Dominie comes from the Latin 'dominus' meaning 'master' and the schoolmaster, kirk minister and doctor were the three most respected figures in Livingston Village life.

Originally built as the manse for the minister at Tulloch United Free Kirk after the Disruption of the Church of Scotland in 1843, this very attractive stone-built 'L' shaped Victorian villa was later named 'Birchfield.' This pretty tree-branched framed view was taken in 1962. When Tulloch Kirk, which stood to the east of Livingston Village, was demolished, three of its fine Victorian stained glass windows were saved and now form an attractive feature in St Andrew's Church, at Deans.

'Morven' is one of several traditionally Scottish cottages in Livingston Village. This photograph was taken in 1962, by which time reception of both BBC and commercial television, in the form of STV, had been available for about six years. Separate aerials were, however, still required, as can be seen from the two attached to the chimney breast above the dormer windows.

Sadly, not all of Livingston Village's old houses survived to be appreciated in the modern town. This ivy-clad ruin was demolished shortly after this picture was taken in 1962. With foresight it could have been preserved and later restored to form a fine traditional home.

Charlesfield Lodge, with its castellated tower, was unfortunately demolished shortly before the creation of the New Town Corporation which, from 1962 onwards, carefully protected and safeguarded all of the district's historic buildings. Charlesfield stood on the south side of the River Almond and this view shows it from the south-east. The house was built between 1795 and 1798, during the time of the Napoleonic War, by the Revd Thomas Hardy. The minister sold it almost as soon as it was completed and later it was purchased by Henry Raeburn, the son of the well-known Scottish artist. Raeburn possessed a large collection of his father's paintings and a visitor to Charlesfield described it as 'crowded with perfection.'

Surrounded by its sturdy stone wall, Bloom House was built originally as the home for the owner of Bloom Farm, whose fields were devoured as housing land by the New Town. This was the second time that Bloom Farm had lost its agricultural land: during the Second World War its fields were also requisitioned to use as the site for a large temporary Prisoner of War Camp. Despite the ongoing hostilities between Great Britain and Germany, the local people treated the prisoners well and, on several occasions, welcomed them to sing at services in the village kirk. The prisoners were sent out each day under guard to work on local farms. Later, when they were transferred to another Prisoner of War Camp at Morton Hall on the southern outskirts of Edinburgh, the Germans formed an orchestra and asked to be allowed to return to perform a concert in Livingston to express their thanks for the hospitality which they had received from the villagers. As well as the POWs, the war years between 1939 and 1945 also brought an influx of children to Livingston as the village was designated a safe area to receive evacuees from the threat of enemy bombing raids on Glasgow and Edinburgh. Again, many friendships were formed and some villagers continued to correspond with their childhood city friends for many years after peace was declared.

Livingston Village used to be home to many craftsmen, and in this picture by the well-known local photographer Robert Braid, the carpenter with his saw tucked under his arm, is seen chatting to the blacksmith with his hammer, outside the smiddy. The blacksmith, puffing away at his clay pipe, was also a good farrier who made iron shoes for the many horses in the district.

This fine photograph is simply captioned, 'A Livingston Station shale miner pictured while home on leave during the Second World War. He served with his regiment in France.' Unfortunately his name is not given. Presumably he is pictured with his wife and toddler. The little one must now be almost sixty years old.

The old Livingston Village shop was later converted into a hairdressing salon. In the past the village also had its own dairy which, in addition to milk and butter, also sold its own home-cured ham, a 'sweetie' shop , a fish and chip shop, a bicycle repair and hire shop and the post office, whose premises still stand on the opposite side of the street. Livingston Village Post Office was where photographer Robert Braid had his tiny darkroom under the stairs. His wife was the village postmistress. Braid produced and printed thousands of postcards in the days before telephones, when they were the commonest way of sending messages. While many photographers in other Scottish towns and villages also published postcard series, it was Baird who came up with the novel idea of adding actors to the views and turning out series of cards telling a simple story, usually with a touch of humour.

The horses included many Clydesdales like this one, standing patiently in its field next to the little white-harled cottage, which used to stand in Livingston Village.

'The Sweep Gets A Job,' was one of Robert Braid's most popular series of comic cards and as in many of his other series he used his relatives and friends in Livingston Village as his actors to 'star' in them. In 'The Sweep Gets A Job', Livingston Village postman Mr Imrie, who was a chimney sweep in his spare time, played the part of the sweep. According to Scottish tradition sweeps were considered lucky, and brides on their way to their wedding ceremonies loved to meet a sweep, but in his cards Baird made his sweep unlucky, something signposted in this the first card in the series by the scullery maid pointing to the upside down horseshoe. The scullery maid doing the weekly washing was conveniently played by village postmistress, Mrs Braid.

In the second card of the five card series, the careless chimney sweep carried away a pair of voluminous, spotlessly white, linen pantalettes, which had been hung out to dry on the washing line, caught on the end of his long soot covered brushes, to move the story forward to the next picture.

Even Mr Braid's young daughter, as well as his wife, was pressed into service in the following picture, entitled 'The Sweep Comes To Grief.' She can be seen peeping out of the door of the house from which the mistress of the house has just appeared. The mistress is thought to have been portrayed by Mrs Mary Bishop, whose daughter Mrs Shields later lived in the village in Bloom Place. The scullery maid walloping the sweep was considered to add extra humour to the scene in the days long before women's liberation was even a gleam in a feminist's eye and long before equal rights.

The Livingston Village policeman played himself in the fourth postcard entitled 'The Strong Arm of the Law'. Braid's photographs were always rich in detail and in this one the big wooden wash tub with the washing board sticking out from the top is strategically placed. Notice also the large wicker-work clothes basket in which the washing would be carried to the washing line to be pegged out to dry.

With his finger pointing significantly to the upside-down horseshoe on the brick wall of the wash-house to indicate that his luck has truly run out, the sweep is marched away by the Livingston Village policeman. The sunlight slanting down the rear wall to frame the mistress and the maid is a reminder that to begin with Braid took all of his postcard pictures out of doors and even developed his photographic plates outdoors by sun light. When his wife retired as postmistress in 1938, the year before the outbreak of the Second World War, the business was acquired by Mr John Shields, who also inherited thousands of Braid's glass plates. They were tightly packed in small wooden boxes stacked around the walls of the garage. Mr Braid drove thousands of miles all over Scotland taking his picture postcard views and, as a keen motorist, had dug a car inspection pit in the middle of the garage floor. Mr Shield did not own a car and so decided to fill in the inspection pit, and not realising the interest which they would have created in the future, used the boxes of glass plates as handy material with which to do so. Thus ended Livingston's early challenge to become Scotland's answer to California's Hollywood!

Almost three thousand, five hundred miles across the Atlantic Ocean in the USA, there is another Livingston Village, not in California but in Upper New York State.

Two

Lords, Lairds and the Leisured Elite

The ease of access which the coming of the toll road provided and the sheltered setting which Livingston enjoyed on the shores of the River Almond combined to attract Edinburgh city business and professional families to acquire estates in the area. A fine new manor house was built by the Murray family to replace the old Livingston Peel tower and it was later purchased by Sir James Cunningham, whose descendants lived there for around a century. He was succeeded in 1767 by his eldest son, Sir William. After a military career, during which he rose to the rank of captain in the Duke of Buccleuch's Southern regiment of Fencibles, he became Member of Parliament for Linlithgowshire, as West Lothian was then called.

During the long periods when the House of Commons was in recess, Sir William's main interest was fox-hunting, which he did regularly with both the Linlithgow and Stirlingshire Hunt and with the new Caledonian Hunt of which he was one of the twelve founder members. Sir William built kennels for the hounds of the Linlithgow and Stirlingshire Hunt on his estate. They were sited on the west side of the road from Mid Calder to Pumpherston and became known locally as the Dog Houses. As well as kennels for the hounds, the building included a house for the huntsman, who looked after them. One evening the huntsman shut the hounds up for the night and as was his custom walked to one of the inns in Mid Calder, where he enjoyed a refreshment. On this occasion, however, he had a drink or two too many and in the wee small hours of the morning stumbled home very drunk. Very much under the influence he missed the entrance to his house and in the darkness stumbled instead into the kennels. The noise woke the hounds, who set upon the intruder and bit him so severely that he was killed. Next morning, according to local tradition, all that was found of the luckless fellow were two pieces of material from his clothes, his two big leather top boots and a rickle of bones on which the hounds were chewing with satisfaction!

On a more cheerful note, Sir William Cunningham also delighted in entertaining at Livingston Place. During his first and second marriages, lines of landaus, broughams and other horse-drawn carriages often lined the driveway to the big house as his guests dined and danced the night away. Livingston Place's role in the life of Scotland's high society, however, came to an abrupt end in 1828 when Sir William died at his London town house. The estate was then purchased by the fourth Earl of Rosebery who was already established in the recently-built magnificent new Dalmeny House on the shores of the River Forth and had no wish to move home. Livingston Place therefore remained empty for a number of years until it was decided to demolish it during the 1840s. Other well known families, however, continued to live in Livingston and several of their stately homes at Alderston, Bankton, Dechmont, Howden, Limefield, Murieston and Newpark still survive.

Fig. 11.—View of Alderston House from N.

Alderstone House is situated midway between Livingston town centre and Bellsquarry. The house was built by lawyer Patrick Kinloch, who practised as an advocate at the Court of Session in Edinburgh. His family had bought Alderstone Estate in 1556 and the house was completed in 1626. It is a very typical Scottish L-shaped three storey mansion and is listed as a 'category A' building of architectural and historic importance.

When the New Statistical Account of Scotland was published in the 1840s, Alderstone belonged to Mr William Bruce and it is recorded that as one of the richest rate payers in the area, he was required to contribute the then considerable sum of £364 per annum as the largest share of the stipend of the parish minister. In more modern times Alderstone was acquired by the Whitelaw family whose most famous member, Willie Whitelaw, became British Home Secretary.

A feature of the grounds of Alderstone House is its doo'cote. This intriguing old building, seen here when it fell into a state of disrepair, is an interesting reminder of the years before the Agricultural Revolution of the mid-1700s, when lack of root vegetables such as turnips for winter fodder meant that most cows and sheep had to be slaughtered each autumn, leaving a great shortage of fresh food. To compensate for this Scottish lairds were encouraged to build dove cotes or doo'cotes, as they were known, in which to keep pigeons, ready for their cooks to turn into casseroles and very tasty pies. This picture of the doo'cote without its roof allows the tiers of nesting boxes in the tall interior to be clearly seen.

The Alderstone doo'cote has now been beautifully restored. It is classified as a 'lectern doo'cote' and its steeply sloping grey slate roof faces south to allow the pigeons to sunbathe on fine days. Directly below the roof are the pigeon-holes, which allowed the birds to fly in and out and from which the expression, 'pigeon-holed' is derived. The stone ridge or rope, running round the sides and front of the building very effectively kept rats and other predators out as their back bones were not flexible enough to allow them to climb round it. Human predators were excluded by the small door which was kept locked at all times, except when the scullery lad was sent to wring the necks of a dozen or so plump little squabs, as the young pigeons were known, for the cook to bake in a pie. The small round window was to allow in some light and inside the doo'cote was equipped with a ladder, which swivelled on a central pole so that even the highest of the stone nesting boxes could be reached.

The doo'cotes at Howden House, mentioned in the previous caption, can be clearly seen tucked into the eaves at either end of the stable block, in the days when it was still used for agricultural purposes.

The stable block at Howden has now been restored and converted into an attractive and well-equipped theatre and art gallery where many professional and amateur shows are presented. It is also available as a conference centre.

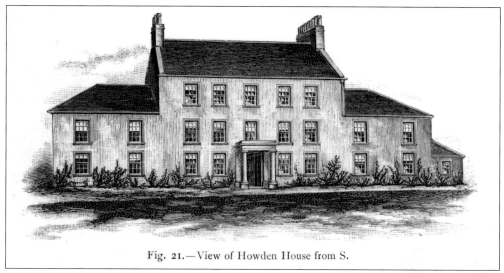

Fig. 21.—View of Howden House from S.

Mentions of Howden Estate occur as early as the fifteenth century when the lands belonged to the Douglas family of Pumpherston. During the seventeenth century it was the property of the Bryce family, and during the 1930s was purchased in turn by two Edinburgh lawyers, Mr Inglis and Mr Wilson. The house was completed in 1795 and as befits that date is typically Georgian in style, with symmetrical two-storey wings on either side of the three-storey high central block. Built of stone, with a grey slate roof, its walls are harled, that is rough cast, to protect them from the ravages of Scottish winter weather. In the year of its completion, Howden was the scene of a high-society wedding, when Dr James Gregory, who discovered the great nursery cure-all, Gregory's Mixture, was married in the drawing-room.

In the nineteenth century Howden House was bought by the Revd James White, whose sister Charlotte was the wife of Henry Raeburn of nearby Charlesfield Lodge and daughter-in-law of the renowned Scottish painter. Later, in Victorian times, it became the home of Agnes Young, daughter of the mineral oil magnate, James 'Paraffin' Young, when she married James Edward Stoddart, the nephew of her father's business partner, Edward Meldrum of Dechmont House. In 1964 the Carnegie Trust gave a grant of £12,000 to convert Howden House from offices for the Ministry of Agriculture and Fisheries into a community centre for the New Town.

Knightsridge House takes its name from the fact that the lands on which it stands belonged originally to the Knights of the Order of St John of Jerusalem, who had their Scottish headquarters fifteen miles to the north in the Bathgate Hills at Torphichen. This attractive red sandstone late Georgian mansion was built in 1831, replacing an earlier mansion erected in 1710. It is interesting to note that, while expensive red sandstone was imported to the area for the construction of the house, its farm steading and pigeon doo'cote were constructed more economically of locally found cream sandstone.

Murieston Castle stood on the site of what is now one of Livingston's largest private housing developments. It is probable that the place name is derived from the 'toun' or township of servants' cottages which grew up around Murray's Castle. This is the only illustration of the castle known to exist, but even in the ruinous condition into which it had deteriorated before it was drawn, several of its defensive features can still be distinguished, including its fortified tower and its arrow slit windows. Murieston Castle is mentioned in the First Statistical Account of Scotland published during the 1790s. It is described as an 'uninhabited fortified peel tower.'

Fig. 30.—View of Murieston Castle from N W.

Fig. 27.—View of Murieston House from S E.

By the time of the Second Statistical Account of Scotland, published in the 1840s, Murieston Castle had entirely disappeared, its stones probably looted to construct farm buildings in the district. On its site had arisen this imposing Georgian mansion house with its impressive front entrance and the windows of its spacious rooms set symmetrically on either side of the doorway. It was the home of Mr James M. Hog.

Fig. 14.—View of Bankton House from S.

Bankton House, after which a whole area of the New Town in the Dedridge District has been named, along with a primary school, still stands and has been converted into a restaurant. This very attractive mansion consists of a two-storey high central block with single-storey wings. The porticoed entrance adds interest to the frontage.

DECHMONT HOUSE

Scottish Baronial-style Dechmont House, with its witches-hat turreted tower and mock fortified battlements, was the home of Edward Meldrum, the partner of James 'Paraffin' Young.

Limefield House was for many years the home of James 'Paraffin' Young. Here Young entertained his former classmate at Glasgow's Anderson Institute, now the University of Strathclyde, and lifelong friend, the famous Scottish missionary and explorer David Livingstone. During his stay Livingstone delighted Young's large family by building a miniature African tribal village with thatched roofed rondavels in the grounds. He also dammed the stream which flows though the grounds to recreate the Victoria Falls, which he was the first European to discover. The little sycamore sapling which Livingstone planted on his visit to Limefield still stands in the grounds and dominates the garden. The house has been used as a retirement home but is now no longer deemed suitable for this purpose and there has been much local concern about finding a fitting purpose for it.

Three
The Shale Oil Bonanza

James 'Paraffin' Young had actually retired and handed over his shale-oil empire to the management of his eldest son, before mining began within the boundaries of what now forms the territory of Livingston New Town. It was in 1884 that Deans Crude Oil Works were opened by one of Young's rival firms, the West Lothian Oil Company, and the following year sixteen cottages known as the Deans Rows were built to accommodate their workers.

Only eight years later, in the fierce competition which existed in the Scottish shale-oil industry, the Dean Crude Oil Works were closed as inefficient, only to be purchased the following year by Pumpherston Oil Company. The Pumpherston Company redesigned the works and reopened them in 1897. They remained in production until 1949 and were finally demolished in 1954. The Deans Crude Oil Works required 1,000 tons of shale a day to feed their retorts and various shale mines were operated at different times below the area covered by the New Town. Deans No.1 and Deans No.2, which was known as Caputhall Mine, were worked until 1906. Deans No.3, which ran below where the NEC electronics factory now stands, was nicknamed Starlaw Mine after the hamlet which formerly stood on this site. It continued in production until 1920.

By this time the shale companies had merged into Scottish Oils to tackle the growing competition from overseas sources of oil but, despite this timely move, the last mines in Livingston – Deans No.5 and No.6 mines – were finally closed. The Deans Crude Oil Works and its associated mines created many jobs for the inhabitants of Livingston Station. It took its name from the opening of the railway line operated by the Edinburgh & Bathgate Railway Company, which had been incorporated by Act of Parliament in 1846 and begun services on 12 November 1849.

There were six passenger stations on the route that connected with the main Glasgow-to-Edinburgh line at Ratho. Only one year short of its centenary, Livingston railway station was closed in 1948, although passenger trains continued to pass through it operating from Bathgate to Edinburgh until these LNER services were also withdrawn in 1956.

The story of Livingston's passenger-rail services, however, has had a happy ending because it now once again has direct services from Livingston South Station to both Glasgow and Edinburgh and from Livingston North Station to Bathgate and Edinburgh. Fast diesel engines have replaced the old steam ones and the journey to Edinburgh Waverley takes only twenty minutes, providing the residents of Livingston with one of the best commuter train services in Scotland.

James 'Paraffin' Young, the founder of the Scottish mineral oil industry and the man who had the most dramatic effect on the Livingston area during Victorian times, was born in Glasgow in 1811. Young studied chemistry at the city's Anderson College and proved such a good student that he became assistant to Professor Thomas Graham and later Professor in his own right at University College, London. From the academic world he was attracted into the world of industry and, recognising the increased demand for oil created by the Industrial Revolution, sought to find a new source for this vital product. His quest brought him to West Lothian to exploit the oil-rich Torbanehill Mineral. This proved in short supply and so he turned instead to using the less oil-bearing, but far more plentiful shale rock, seams of which lay below where Livingston now stands. Young set such high standards for his product that from being considered a dangerous substance, oil gained a reputation for its safety and his new improved paraffin lamps became accepted as the best way to light homes from cottages to castles throughout the country, thus his famous nickname. As an entrepreneur, Young proved so successful that he felt able to retire from active business in 1866 and returned to the academic world studying pure science and dedicating a chair at what is now Strathclyde University. He died in 1883.

The shale-oil industry forever changed the landscape of the Livingston district and the famous Five Sisters Bing is now the area's most famous landmark, enjoying A-category status as an ancient monument and achieving a heraldic first by appearing on West Lothian Council's coat of arms, approved by the Lord Lyon King Of Arms. The Five Sisters overlook the Freeport discount shopping precinct and there have been various suggestions to construct a cable car to one of the summits and establish a dry ski slope as an attraction for visitors. The word 'bing' is derived from the Gaelic 'Bein' or, more familiarly, 'Ben', meaning a mountain, and is indeed a graphic description for these man-made hills, which dominate the Livingston scene.

4217 Deans Oil Works, Livingston Station.

Although the Five Sisters with their peaked summits soaring skywards are the bings chosen to be preserved for posterity as an ancient monument, the bings which used to surround Livingston were more usually pink, plateau-topped monsters, such as this massive one which rose steeply behind Deans Oil Works. The lone car parked in front of the work's offices, which gives a good impression of the height of the bing, belonged to the works manager.

The two tall chimney stacks were a well-known Livingston landmark.

Deans Oil Works closed in 1949 and the buildings were demolished in 1954. For a while after the surface buildings were removed, the chimneys remained as a gaunt reminder of the shale-oil industry's prosperous past, until two years later in 1956 they were dynamited in two spectacular explosions.

This action photograph shows the explosive charge being detonated at the base of the second of the chimneys to be felled.

The second of the Deans chimneys plunged earthwards in a billowing cloud of dust. The huge bing behind it was also later removed.

YOUNG'S PARAFFIN LIGHT & MINERAL OIL COMPANY. LIMITED.
ADDIEWELL WORKS. WEST CALDER. SCOTLAND.

When the Scottish mineral oil industry was at its peak, the chimneys at Deans were only two among a forest of mighty lums, which all spewed out their thick acrid smoke across the Livingston landscape, as shown in this poster produced to advertise Young's new oil refinery at Addiewell. The construction of the Addiewell Works began in 1866, the year in which Young retired from active participation in the business. It was a very memorable year for the inventor as it was also the occasion on which his long-lasting friend from their student days together at Glasgow's Anderson Institute, the by then world-famous explorer Sir David Livingstone came to stay with him during a furlough from his missionary work in Africa. Young took the opportunity to invite his celebrity guest to perform the ceremony of laying the first stone at the new oil works and repaid Livingston by financing much of his work in the Dark Continent.

Petrol produced from Scottish mineral oil was marketed appropriately as Scotch and dispensed from distinctive thistle-topped pumps such as this one.

A rival brand of petrol produced form Scottish shale was sold as Ross Petrol and was manufactured at the refinery of James Ross & Company at Philpstoun.

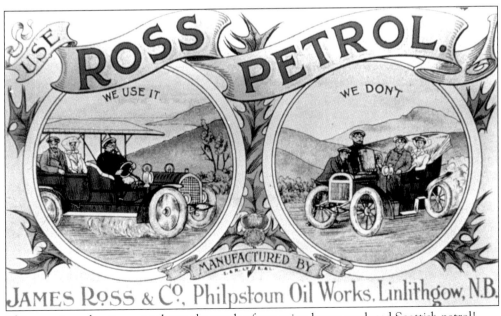

This amusing advertisement shows the result of not using home produced Scottish petrol!

The local motoring scene moves on into the 1920s with this photograph of a car filling up at the pumps at the well-known Pratts Garage at Raw Camp, with one of the shale bings in the background. The hoarding on the roadside verge advertises Gold Flake cigarettes, which seems appropriate considering the scene in the following picture.

Look what the smartly uniformed chauffeur is holding between his fingers in this happy holiday weekend photograph, taken at Pratts Garage on the edge of the New Town near East Calder in the 1920s, before the danger of smoking near petrol filling pumps had apparently been recognized! The open-topped tourer with the bonnet up was however happily covered by the AA. In addition to catching a wealth of detail about the car with its large headlights, separate sidelights, and spare wheel at the ready at the front of the running-board, the photographer also captured many fascinating fashion details from the dashing young man in plus fours to the older gentleman in his black bowler hat and the young apprentice in his dungarees. The two lady passengers in the car are both wearing cloche hats.

As well as petrol, Scottish shale oil was used in the manufacture of many other products from paint to mothballs and James Young was famed for finding uses for his product. Its most celebrated use, however, was as a fuel for paraffin lamps, as illustrated by this poster. Many of Young's safety paraffin lamps, which were designed to eliminate explosions, were works of considerable artistic beauty as well. Notice how many gold medals the Livingston-produced paraffin was awarded at industrial shows not just in Great Britain but also abroad.

Obtaining the bluish, slate-like shale rock was back-breaking work for the men who worked underground in the shale mines. However, they always claimed they enjoyed better conditions than coal miners, as larger seams meant greater headroom and less danger of explosions from deadly methane gas or firedamp, as it was often known. This photograph shows two of the miners working at the shale face, with the furthest away one drilling a charge.

A close-up view of drilling a hole to place an explosive charge in the shale face.

The large amounts of explosives required by the shale-mining industry were produced at Camulty Explosive Works. It was situated in a dip in the hills close to the former village of Oakbank at Harburn, not far from where the well-known golf course is sited today. From there the explosives were distributed by horse-drawn cart, not direct to the shale mines but to the recently established Co-operative Stores. These community-owned shops then sold the explosive in blue paper bags to the miners, who were responsible for buying their own supplies. There are many stories of how the miners took it home and stored it beneath their box beds in the rows, until the shift, when they required it to set a charge at the shale face.

The dangerous work of manufacturing the dynamite at Camulty was carried out by a mainly female staff, seen here photographed with the work's male managers and office staff. The Camulty Explosive Factory closed during the 1920s.

The introduction of electric power to the underground workings of the shale mines made it easier to drill the holes required to set the charges in the rock face. The miner is wearing a metal helmet and safety lamp but no eye protection or ear protectors to save his hearing from the deafening blast as the shale came crashing down.

This photograph of working conditions underground in the shale industry was taken at Dedridge Mine.

Two of the miners at Dedridge Mine are seen working at the rock face, while a third in the foreground shovels the shale ready to load it into one of the hutches.

One of the shale workers tends a heavily laden hutch.

To begin with, pit ponies were used to provide underground motive power in the shale mines. Long-time Livingston Village resident Jock Gibb was the son of the ostler in charge of the underground stables at Deans No.5 Mine. As soon as he was fourteen years old, he left school and his father found him a job as a pony lad. There were thirty-five ponies in the stables far beneath the surface and each lad was responsible for one of them. Mr Gibb described his first pony as 'a right wise beast. His name was Star and I used to take him a tattie, but after munching his potato he also always used to love having a wee bit of my piece at break time each morning. Most of the miners were very fond of their ponies and took them tidbits every day. As a wee pony Star only pulled one hutch at a time and if he decided it was too heavy laden, he was quite capable of tipping the tail chain and getting out of it. After a few months, I was promoted to a much bigger and stronger beast called Bob. He was almost as big as a horse an could pull several hutches fully laden. As the ostler, my father was very strict about the condition the pit ponies were kept in and always watched they were never taken into too low a working. He was very proud of the many certificates which the Scottish Society for the prevention of Cruelty to Animals presented to Deans Number Five Mine.'

Once a year the shale mine ponies were brought to the surface for their summer holidays. Despite working underground for most of the year, the ponies were not blind as many people thought, but during their first day or two on the surface had to be blinkered to protect their eyes from the unaccustomed sunlight. Each year during their annual holidays the ponies were taken to Linlithgow to make an appearance at the West Lothian County Agricultural Show and were always a popular attraction. The last shale mine ponies were brought to the surface and retired in April 1958.

The shale-mining industry continued to use pit ponies until the 1950s for underground transport. On the surface, by contrast, it used many of the most modern means of motive power, as this view of the overhead haulage system at Dedridge Mine shows. It carried the loads of shale to the oil refinery.

This close-up view shows the fully laden hutches leaving Dedridge Mine on their journey to the oil refinery at Oakbank.

The overhead haulage system was designed and manufactured in Germany. Here German engineers are seen putting final touches to it at the point where it spanned the A71 Edinburgh to Kilmarnock road. This is now one of the busiest roads in the Livingston area, but before the First World War when the aerial transport system was erected and this photograph was taken, the only traffic consisted of two horse-drawn carts.

This other view of the overhead railway shows it crossing the A71 road. The steel pylons originally bore plaques bearing details of the German manufacturers of the Livingston overhead haulage system, but these were removed at the start of the First World War in 1914 in case they provoked any angry incidents.

For most of its route the Livingston overhead haulage system travelled over open agricultural land.

When the overhead railway came near to a road or a farm, safety nets were strung below it as can be seen in this photograph.

This is how the overhead haulage system used to look at Dedridge.

Industry and farming met where the overhead haulage system crossed the beautifully thatched haystacks at Glebe Farm. The name Glebe Farm is a reminder that these lands were originally granted to the local minister and that he was expected to use these fields to grow food to supplement his basic annual stipend. This attractive view of the country comes to town was taken in the autumn at the close of the harvest season. The successful gathering in of the harvest was always marked in Livingston with a harvest thanksgiving service in the kirk and each of the local farmers was also expected to reward his workers and their families with a harvest home party and dance. It is now many years since haystacks were seen in the fields around Livingston. As soon as it is cut, the hay crop is now stored in large round circular black plastic bags in which to slowly turn into silage for use as winter fodder. This system is very practical but the space-age looking black bags have none of the rural beauty of the old-fashioned hay stacks.

This photograph provides a detailed view of the overhead haulage system.

This stark shot shows the haulage system at New Farm Mine, Dedridge.

These hutches laden with shale ore were pictured as they came to the surface at Dedridge Mine.

An excellent view of the incline at Dedridge Mine.

From the oil works at Oakbank the railway was built to transport tanker loads of oil.

On their way home from school local laddies often followed the railway track as an easy route to their houses in the miners rows at Oakbank.

When they grew up, the wee boys in the previous photograph would mostly follow their fathers into the shale-oil industry like these employees at Pumpherston Works, who posed for this picture with the refinery manager in his three piece suit and collar and tie.

By modern standards even the manual workers look formally dressed, as shown here by this employee of Oakbank Oil Works who posed for the cameraman, with his 'doo-lander' flat cap, so called because it was so big a pigeon could land on it !

John Roberts, the son of work's manager Edward Roberts, is seen in this view taken at Deans Oil Works.

One of the largest of the shale-oil developments was on the east side of the New Town at Pumpherston Oil Works. The huge site was first developed in 1883 by William Fraser, who had previously been a manager at Uphall. At its height, the works covered 1,200 acres.

Process workers at Deans Oil Works.

Getting rid of the waste shale ash was always a problem for the shale-oil industry. The massive flat topped bing where it accumulated can be seen in this photograph of Pumpherston Oil Works.

Steam rises from one of the retorts where the shale ore was converted into oil at Pumpherston. The Scottish shale-oil industry was considered so vital to the war effort during the First World War that details of the oil works were omitted from the maps of the period in case they fell into the possession of the enemy and were used to assist Zeppelin air attacks.

Tall chimneys loomed high over the railway lines at Pumpherston Oil Works.

This photograph shows Westwood Mine. The worst tragedy in the history of the Scottish shale-oil industry occurred at nearby Burngrange Mine on 10 January 1947. Seventy-six men were working underground on the afternoon shift, when, six hours into it, at 8 p.m. two explosions rocked the underground workings. The blasts blew the three men nearest to them off their feet. As the billowing cloud of dust slowly cleared, two of them picked themselves up, but the third miner lay unconscious on the floor of the mine workings. He died as he was being carried on a stretcher to the mine surface. When news of the explosions reached the manager in his office, he found it so hard to believe that Westwood, with its excellent safety record until that day, could have been devastated in such a way, that instead of calling the mine rescue service immediately, he summoned the overman and together they went bravely below ground to sum up the damage and see what aid they could provide.

The mine manager and his overman quickly took in the terrible tragedy of the situation as they saw that the blasts had shattered the underground workings at Burngrange, setting off a fire, and that fourteen of the men were cut off beyond the blaze. They raced back to the surface and from the mine office summoned the mine rescue team and all of the other emergency services. Sadly, there was little they could do. It took them four days to extinguish the flames and when, on 14 January, they finally reached the trapped miners they found them all dead. They had collapsed where they had been working. Only two had slight burns, but all fourteen had been overwhelmed and suffocated by deadly carbon monoxide gas. The fortieth anniversary of the tragedy was marked by the unveiling of a plaque bearing the names of those who died: Henry Cowie, David Carroll, William Carroll, George Easton, John Fairley, William Findlay, Anthony Gaughan, William Greenock, Thomas Heggie, John Lightbody, John McGarty, James McCauley, David Muir, Samuel Pake and William Ritchie.

As shale was generally found at shallower depths than coal, it was usually dug from sloping mines rather than deep pits as here at Westwood Mine.

The Five Sisters Bing dominates the scene on the western side of Livingston.

Oakbank Railway Engine No.2 is pictured here at East Pumpherston.

The squad of workmen who demolished Camulty Explosives Factory in September 1931.

Another squad of demolishers, this time the men who knocked down Deans Oil Works in 1954. The Scottish shale-oil industry struggled on under ever increasing competition from imported oil from the Persian Gulf and other foreign sources for another eight years until 1962. If the government had chosen to save the Scottish shale-oil industry by granting it tax relief, it could have continued to provide much needed employment because there were still adequate reserves of shale waiting to be exploited. The industry could not compete on cost grounds as it was a manually intensive and thus expensive way to produce fuel. The same cost factor also closed the shale-oil industry in Australia. In other parts of the world such as California, on the other hand, experiments with obtaining oil from shale by burning it underground and pumping the resulting oil to the surface have succeeded in cutting costs. If it follows this example, perhaps someday a new modernized shale-oil industry will be reborn.

The retort where the shale ore was burned to produce oil at the Deans Oil Works at the moment when it was demolished using explosives.

A second later the huge retort was reduced to a pile of rubble revealing more of the buildings of Deans Oil Works, shortly before they too were demolished.

The vast plateau-like pink bing belonging to Deans Oil Works remained for a time as a last memorial to the Scottish oil industry, but it too has now been removed and the area landscaped.

Big Ben, Almond Valley Heritage Centre's popular Clydesdale horse, pulled this vintage lamp-oil wagon through the streets of Livingston on this snowy winter day. The Heritage Centre is the official museum of the Scottish shale-oil industry and its collection of exhibits provides excellent coverage of Scotland's oil boom years.

Four

Life in the Rows

The rows were the long, low lines of houses hurriedly constructed to house the large numbers of workers required to labour in the shale mining industry during Livingston's oil bonanza. Mostly built of brick but sometimes of stone, the rows were built as cheaply as possible by the oil companies and rented to their employees. These economic homes formed practically all of the housing available in places like Livingston Station, Oakbank, Addiewell and Pumpherston.

From the outside the long serried lines of rows looked identical, each with two rooms set on either side of the centrally placed front door, but inside the miners' and oil workers' wives prided themselves on how they managed to give their humble homes some individuality. Focal point of the living room was the long black-leaded iron kitchen range which heated the row and provided a means of cooking and of heating the water for the miners' baths, when they 'loused' at the end of their shifts. To begin with, the rows did not have any piped water supply so all of the gallons of water required each day had to be painstakingly fetched from standpipes in the streets. Sanitation was equally primitive with dry closets or privies at the back of each block, usually shared by many families. Despite these deprivations, the womenfolk were famed for their cleanliness and liked to decorate the living rooms with ornaments, among the favourites being china 'wally' dogs, always sold in pairs one facing right and the other left so that they could sit looking inward at the end of the mantle shelf. The other room in the row was where the whole family slept, the mother and father often in a box bed built into the wall, while the children occupied trestle beds, which folded away and were stored in a cupboard under the box bed when not in use. The rows were very much self-contained little communities and any stranger who ventured into them was watched with deep suspicion, the first family to spot the intruder quickly ensuring that all the other inhabitants of the block were alerted by knocking on the intervening walls between their homes. Social life in the rows centred on the miners' institutes, early forms of community centres, partially funded by the employers and partially by a levy which the government imposed on every ton of shale which was mined. Facilities at the institutes included halls, meeting rooms and libraries as well as sports facilities ranging from indoor billiards to outdoor lawn bowling greens and sometimes even tennis courts. During the boom years of the Scottish mineral oil industry, relationships between employers and men were generally positive but by the 1920s and 1930s, as the effect of ever increased foreign competition squeezed profit margins, there were many strikes and the institutes were often used as soup-kitchens to feed the starving families. Happier times were when the institutes housed annual summer gala day teas and provided a setting for family events such as wedding receptions. The rows had a way of life all of their own and, although they have now almost all been demolished, many older inhabitants still have vivid memories of what it was like to grow up and live in these crowded streets.

Miners' rows lined the Main Street in Livingston Station. The one nearest the camera was called Fisherrow. Some villagers claim that it got this unusual name from the fact that its first inhabitants came from the coastal fishing villages seeking work. It seems more likely, however, that it was given this description as a nickname because it was at this spot in Main Street that the fishwives of Fisherrow near Musselburgh sold their fresh haddock, cod and herring on their weekly visits, when they travelled out by train from Edinburgh.

While a fresh bit of fish made a nice wee change once a week, most of the miners much preferred stews and steak pies and butcher meat was delivered to the rows in Livingston Station, and the other shale mining villages in the Livingston area, by G. Halliday & Son Family Butchers who, as well as a shop in West Calder, operated this 'Dad's Army' style motor van complete with porthole-shaped side windows. Notice the wicker delivery basket perched high on the roof. The butcher in his striped apron has the strap of his leather moneybag slung over his shoulder and his delivery boy has a scarlet Flanders poppy in his button hole. Like the butcher he is wearing a flat cloth cap and leather boots, very different from the way a youth of his age would be dressed nowadays.

Private traders like the fishwives and Mr Halliday the butcher always had to compete against the local Co-operative Society. Like Mr Halliday's shop, it had its headquarters in neighbouring West Calder, but had branch stores in all of the shale mining villages. This one in Livingston Station first opened in 1904 and this photograph of it and its staff was taken in 1925. When it first opened in Livingston Station the 'Store' had only 100 members and turnover for the first year of trading was £3,030, but twenty-one years later membership was four hundred and thirty and its business totalled £26,767. As well as groceries sold by the three white apron-clad male members of staff, the 'Store' also supplied the requirements of the residents of Livingston Station for items of drapery such as blankets and sheets, and clothing from thick woollen long john underpants and semmit vests for the miners to tightly-laced whalebone stays and Sunday-best hats for their wives. The young women assistants who served in the drapery also came to the door to pose for the photographer when he took this photograph.

By 1962 West Calder Co-operative Society's premises in Livingston Station had been greatly modernised, but the 'Store' was still very much a part of village life and most residents were still members.. Each family had its own Co-op number, and goods were bought not with cash but with small bone discs known as checks, a record of which enabled each family's share of the dividend to be calculated from their purchases. Credit was allowed, but all debts had to be paid up before the end of each quarter. Often it was a great struggle to achieve this, leading to the last few days in each quarter being christened 'The Lord's My Shepherd Week,' as it was often said that God alone knew how some of the members were going to pay up and still manage to feed their families. The week the 'divi' was paid out was the opposite, of course, and a great opportunity for a spending spree!

From the 1960s onwards the might of the Scottish Co-operative movement was challenged by the growth of rival supermarkets. Here pupils are seen carol singing outside a Gateway supermarket at Christmas in 1990. During the past few years the giant supermarkets have launched customer loyalty cards paying at most a dividend of one and a half pence in the pound, a mere fraction of the old Co-op 'divi,' which sometimes reached the dizzy heights of over four shillings for every single pound spent.

Apart from the winter celebration of Christmas and more especially Hogmanay and New Year, the residents of Livingston Station always looked forward to the village's annual summer Gala Day. The Station was colourfully decorated for the occasion and the miners took great pride in building decorative arches such as this impressive triple one, which was erected around 1900. While the menfolk built the wooden frame and covered it with neatly clipped green boxwood, the women and girls made the colourful decorations out of cardboard and crepe paper. New Gala Day outfits were always purchased as can be seen from the fashions worn by the mothers and children in this photograph. As well as the ladies, the girls in their teens wore hats as a sign that they were no longer wee lassies, but now very much grown-ups.

A highlight of every Livingston Station village Gala Day was the procession with the school bairns pictured here marching past the rows in North Street in 1926. The style of the outline of the roofs of the houses is an indication that these rows belonged to the Pumpherston Oil Company, which operated the local shale mines and also the Deans Oil Works. The reward for each child at the end of the procession was a brown paper bag filled with a sausage roll, a cream cookie, an iced cake and a bar of chocolate or sweeties.

This photograph is of a more recent Livingston Station Gala Day, probably in the early 1960s. The pipe band is playing in the background, while the girls prepare for the sports and races. They are still happily turned out for the Gala Day in summer dresses with no denim jeans or sports fashion-wear in sight.

The pretty little daughter of mine manager Mr Dewar is wearing her best white summer dress for this family picture taken during the 1920s, with her mother and father and three brothers in the back garden of their home at 24 Main Street, Livingston Station. Even for this family occasion, Mr Dewar wears a three-piece suit complete with waistcoat and gold watch chain over a white shirt with a stiffly starched white collar. All three of his boys are wearing white shirts with collars and ties under their thick cloth suits, although it is clearly a lovely warm sunny summer day. The two younger ones are in shorts, which were usually worn right up to the school leaving age of fourteen.

Livingston Station residents Mr and Mrs Campbell were photographed outside the door of their brick-built miners row at 18 Main Street in the mid-1920s.

Brother and sister William and Janet Morrison were pictured outside their father Joseph's row at 23 Main Street, Livingston Station in the mid-1920s.

Pictured outside the boilerhouse at Deans Oil Works, this is Mr Joseph Morrison, presumably the father of the children in the previous photograph.

Moving forward two decades, Mr and Mrs Nicolls are pictured here outside their home during the 1940s.

In comparison with crowded miners rows which made up most of the early housing in Livingston Station, the village School House is a spacious detached villa. This picture showing it standing in its tree-lined garden was taken in 1962. It was then the home of the Headmaster of Livingston Station Primary School, later replaced by Deans Primary, which under Headmistress Anne Edgar continues to serve the village. The school now also has a special unit for children with hearing difficulties from all parts of the Livingston area and beyond.

St. Andrews Church in Livingston Station is united with the older kirk in Livingston Village. The three tall stained glass windows seen in this picture came originally from Tulloch United Free Church, and were saved and transferred when it was knocked down after the Second World War.

The notice board at Tulloch United Free Church records that its minister was the Revd John MacRae MA.

The miners rows at Oakbank housed a population of 353 in 1871, but this had almost trebled by the time of the census in 1891, when the figure of 979 was recorded. The rows were all owned by the Oakbank Oil Company and the miners' rents were deducted from their weekly wage packets before they received the money which they had earned.

The miners rows at Oakbank each had their own neatly kept gardens in which the miners grew both vegetables for the soup pot and flowers to decorate their homes. Several of their wives and a large group of their children are seen in this attractive view, which gives Oakbank a distinctly rural look.

Oakbank was nonetheless essentially an industrial village, a fact of which the ever looming shale bing was a constant reminder. The village was very badly affected by the depression of the early 1930s, especially after the shale mine closed in 1932. The rows were all finally demolished in 1984 and the massive bing has since been landscaped. All that now remains of Oakbank is its miners' institute hall and the village bowling green. Both were originally paid for as a result of an Act of Parliament, which levied a small amount for every ton of shale that the miners brought to the surface, to provide these community facilities.

The driver and the conductor with his black leather cash bag waited for passengers to board this early bus, which provided one of the first regular services in the Livingston area. It was owned by Simpson Motor Services.

Simpsons also operated in the Livingston area as Blue Coach Services, as painted on the livery of this 1920s vehicle.

With the compliments of the Season

Heavy snow transformed the Livingston rows into a winter wonderland and this charming view was turned into a very appropriate local Christmas card. Each company had its own style of finishing its rows and the castellated battlement effect on the roofs of these rows suggests that they were occupied by Pumpherston Oil Co. workers.

Five

The New Town

Livingston was dedicated as Scotland's fourth New Town on 16 April 1962, to be 'developed primarily for the purpose of catering for Glasgow oversupply.' The Designation Order went on to state that it was to occupy 6,700 acres of land, partly in the parishes of Mid Calder in the county of Midlothian and partly in two parishes in West Lothian, Uphall and Livingston – deriving its name from the latter. From the outset it was stressed that it was 'to have a proper balance of industrial, commercial, social and other facilities and be properly integrated into the economy of the area.' These were the principles of the great Scottish town planner Patrick Geddes who always stressed the triangle of people, place and work and, by coincidence, planning for Livingston began close to where he had his greatest influence in the Old Town of Edinburgh, when the Livingston Development Commission set up its first temporary offices on the top floor of the *Scotsman* buildings. From there the LDC's Chairman David Lowe, (later knighted) and its first General Manager, Brigadier Arthur Purches, drew up the plans to meet the Secretary of State's demands for 1,000 new houses each year with an ultimate target population of 70,000, which was expected to grow by natural increase to 100,000.

For a variety of reasons, mainly to do with changes in central government policies, Livingston has never grown to this enormous size, reaching 41,500 on its twenty-fifth anniversary and remaining at around that figure ever since. The first new building to be erected in Livingston was the original block of offices to house the LDC's own employees at Livingston Village, for which Secretary of State Michael Noble drove the first pile into the ground in August 1963. In the same year the LDC pulled off its first great coup by attracting the American owned Cameron Iron Works to the New Town and, from then on, achieved a very creditable record in bringing over 400 new industrial, commercial and service companies to provide over 15,000 jobs in Livingston.

From the outset the Livingston master plan was that this should be the first New Town in Britain designed to be a regional centre for the whole of its area. It was also highly successful in regulating the growth and expansion of the New Town, the scheme dictating that it should grow in an orderly fashion from east to west. Therefore, while the first New Town residents were housed in the existing village of Livingston Station, the first major housing development was begun on the hillside at Craigshill. There, in order to meet the government's demand for one thousand new homes every year, a Swedish industrialized method of building was used and the first occupants, Mr and Mrs James Gilchrist and their son Robert moved in on schedule in April 1966 to No.39, Broom Walk. Nearby the first shop was opened by former Rangers goalkeeper Billy Ritchie and Craigshill's covered shopping centre became one of the wonders of the age. Howden East, Ladywell East, Knightsridge, Dedridge, Eilburn, Deans and Carmondean, Deerpark, Bankton and Murieston all followed to become well-known Livingston New Town place names.

The very first resident of the New Town of Livingston was Mr Arnold Dalton, who moved in in 1963. Mr Dalton was the first official employed by Livingston Development Corporation when it appointed him as its Chief Finance Officer. He is pictured here fourteen years later upon his retirement, when he received a presentation from Livingston Development Corporation Chairman, Mr Desmond Misselbrook.

Many strikingly modern new designs were incorporated into the New Town's early houses.

In 1974, twelve years after its inception, Livingston New Town welcomed its 20,000th residents. The happy couple are seen here being received by LDC Chairman, Mr Desmond Misselbrook.

The 20,000th residents were also pictured later with their pet dog as they settled into their new home at Knightsridge.

Livingston continued to grow, and this photograph shows Councillor William Connolly, then Convener of West Lothian District Council and Mr Desmond Misselbrook, Chairman of Livingston Development Corporation, welcoming the Sansom family as occupants of the New Town's 7000th house. Councillor Connolly's work has been commemorated by the naming of West Lothian Library Headquarters as Connolly House in his honour.

The 30,000th resident of the New Town was little Elaine Laughlin, who looked truly delighted when the Chairman of the National Coal Board, Sir Derek Ezra, arrived on her doorstep on her first day in Livingston to present her with this chocolate Easter egg, obviously appreciated by its young recipient much more than flowers would have been. Looking on were her older brother David and her parents, Mr and Mrs George Laughlin.

Mr Misselbrook presented a bouquet to this young mother, Livingston's 25,000th resident.

This impressive aerial view shows how Livingston New Town rapidly spread out across the Almond Valley. Two of the old shale waste bings can be seen in the background.

The ever expanding New Town also required office space, as seen here at Sidlaw House in the town centre. Like other office developments in Livingston it took its name from a range of Scottish hills.

One of the New Town's first residents pushed her baby in its pram past Lammermuir House on this fine early summer day, while a toddler enjoyed riding his bicycle in this carefully landscaped setting.

The landscaping of the gardens surrounding Lomond House had just been completed when this view of the office block was taken to show the excellent spacious facilities which Livingston had to offer.

This more modern view shows the Business Centre in the heart of Livingston. The Livingston Development Corporation took great pride in the millions of trees it succeeded in planting before it handed over control to West Lothian Council, and some of the last saplings which it planted can be seen in front of the Business Centre. (Picture by Dr Arthur Down)

This unusually designed asymmetric suspension bridge leads from Livingston Town Centre across the valley of the River Almond, on whose south shore stands the fine Almondvale Shopping Precinct. Adjacent to the Almondvale Centre is McArthur Park, a designer discount outlet whose attractions also include cafés, a cinema complex and an indoor Ferris wheel, erected to mark the Millennium. (Picture by Dr Arthur Down)

An attractive walkway leads from Livingston Town Centre past the courthouse. (Picture by Dr Arthur Down)

Another busy Livingston town centre attraction is this drive through McDonald's fast food restaurant, whose presence gives a distinctly American feel to the area. In the background behind the hamburger giant's distinctive Golden Arches is Bubbles Leisure and Swimming Complex. (Picture by Dr Arthur Down)

Among the most recent homes, completed shortly before the Millennium, are these ones in Quentin Rise. (Picture by Dr Arthur Down)

Dechmont House is one of the most distinctive homes in Livingston. Standing high on Dechmont Law, the hill on the northern outskirts of the New Town, this fine villa with its distinctly English appearance replaced the original Scottish baronial-style mansion, which stood on this site and which is pictured in an earlier section of this book.

St John's General Hospital in the Howden district of Livingston serves patients from the whole of West Lothian. This unusual view shows some of the wards seen from the south-west corner of its spacious site. The choice of the name St John's for the new hospital, which replaced Bangour, is very appropriate as the Knights of the Order of St John of Jerusalem, the world's oldest order of chivalry, owned lands in this area from medieval times until the Reformation in 1560, as the local place name Knightsridge is a constant reminder. When the new hospital opened it appointed Scotland's first full time hospital chaplain and the post very appropriately went to the Revd Tom Crichton, for twenty-five years minister of Torphichen Kirk, where the Order of St. John had its Scottish headquarters throughout the middle ages and to which farmers and landowners in Livingston had to travel annually to pay their rents. Mr Crichton is now the Prelate to the Order of St John. Many of the doctors, nurses and ancillary staff at the hospital are actively involved in supporting the work of the Order through its Livingston Branch. The beautiful little St John's Chapel provides a quiet retreat for prayer and mediation within this busy modern hospital, whose excellent facilities are much appreciated by the families who make up Livingston's 40,000 inhabitants. (Picture by Dr Arthur Down)

Lauder House, the headquarters of Compaq, is one of many attractive modern developments in Livingston's medical and science campus, whose pleasant working conditions have attracted many young professionals to work here in West Lothian. (Picture by Dr Arthur Down)

The town centre at Almond Vale looked like this as it slowly began to develop.

At the Millennium the town centre looks like this, with the clock tower dominating the busy shopping centre. One of its largest stores is the Asda supermarket and it is in this bustling setting that Livingston Westminster Member of Parliament and British Foreign Secretary, Robin Cook, has set up his weekly surgery so that his local constituents may have ready access to him. The impressively large shopping centre attracts many visitors to Livingston as well as being well patronised by the town's local residents. (Picture by Dr Arthur Down)

At the entrances to Livingston visitors are welcomed by impressive soaring modern sculptures, like this one at the East Roundabout. (Picture by Dr Arthur Down)

This attractive modern hotel and popular family restaurant is also situated at the East Roundabout. (Picture by Dr Arthur Down)

On the south side of Livingston the roundabout is decorated with this witch's hat-like sculpture, which is very appropriate as it is named after Lizzie Brice, who is reputed to have been a local witch who was put to death by being strangled and then burnt at the stake – the savagely severe penalty paid by those found guilty of dabbling in the supernatural in Scotland during the seventeenth century. Over three thousand alleged witches and warlocks were executed in this brutal manner. (Picture by Dr Arthur Down)

Lizzie Brice Roundabout

Exactly how much Livingston has developed in under forty years is shown by this large scale map, helping visitors to gain their bearings when they enter the New Town. (Picture by Dr Arthur Down)

Six
Livingston at School

Many of the overseas employers who have chosen to site their British factories in Livingston have stated that a prime reason for their choice is the well-educated workforce available in the New Town. This is indeed a tribute to Livingston's educational establishments from the town's many nurseries to West Lothian College of Further Education, which provides courses at tertiary level. The Second Statistical Account published in 1843 records that by that time Livingston had two schools and that the 'parochial teacher has the maximum salary, with the legal accommodation of dwelling house, schoolhouse and garden.' The old stone-built former school in Livingston Village was originally built shortly after the Scottish Education Act made school attendance compulsory in 1872. To begin with, it provided both a full primary education and a basic secondary schooling for those of its pupils who stayed on beyond the age of twelve. At the time children as young as five walked all the way to the village school from as far away as Livingston Station.

The first educational facility in Livingston Station took the form of an infant class for five to seven year olds which opened for the first time on 19 September 1905 with forty-two pupils and with Headmistress Edith Fergus in charge. A few years later a purpose-built red brick school was erected at Livingston Station and it enrolled its first pupils on 25 March 1908. The following year its roll was boosted to over 180 when the older children from Livingston Village were also transferred to it, leaving only the first two years of infant pupils to be educated at the village school. This arrangement continued until 1938 when the school in Livingston Village finally closed. The roll at Livingston Station school continued to expand and the School Board agreed to the construction of a much needed extension. By the time it was completed in 1915 there were almost 300 pupils under the school's first headmaster, Mr James Robson, who had until then been the dominie at Livingston Village School.

While primary schools had existed in Livingston for well over a century it was not until the creation of the New Town that it obtained its first purpose-built secondary with the opening of Craigshill High in the mid-1960s. During the same period many new primary schools were rushed up to cope with the ever expanding population which included many young families. Among the schools was Deans Primary, which replaced the old Livingston Station School in 1966, the original building being converted into a community centre. As well as the excellent provision of community education facilities in the New Town, all of its secondary schools, Deans, Inveralmond and James Young High, were specifically designed as community establishments to encourage adults to return to the classroom and improve their qualifications. Livingston's fourth and latest secondary school is St Margaret's Academy, which provides denominational schooling for the town's Roman Catholic population.

The original Williamston Primary School was totally razed to the ground by juvenile vandals. This view shows the replacement Williamston Primary, which was erected on the same site and built of brick in this striking modern style. With its drop-off point in the foreground for parents delivering their children by car, it has a distinctly American appearance to its architecture, with most of its windows protected by being placed on the courtyard side of the building. Like all schools in Livingston it is also protected by an elaborate security system to guarantee pupils and staff safety from intruders. (Picture by Dr Arthur Down)

The first secondary school to be built in the New Town was Craigshill High, whose buildings with their covered playground were considered equally modern when they were erected in the 1960s. Craigshill's popular headmaster was Mr Sandy Pirie, who played a prominent part in community affairs and was a member of the Church of Scotland's National Committee on Education.

Craigshill High has now been replaced by four large community high schools offering an education from the cradle to the grave to all Livingston residents no matter what their age. They are Deans High, James Young High, St Margaret's Academy and Inveralmond High. This view shows the site and modern buildings of the latter, which is situated in the Ladywell district of the town and takes its name from a well dedicated to the Virgin Mary that originally existed in this area. This well is a reminder of the other local spring in New Year's Field, which was reputed to have such curative powers for skin conditions such as scrofula and the dreaded leprosy that pilgrims came from far and wide to bathe in its waters. The waters were said to be particularly effective if applied to the sufferer by the Scottish king, who by tradition came to the well on the first day of the New Year, celebrated in the middle ages at the start of spring. The tradition gives this part of Livingston its unusual local place name.

This is how the buildings and grounds of James Young High School looked almost twenty years ago when photographed in 1982.

The modern premises of Deans Community High School are seen in the background as some of its first year pupils set out on the annual sponsored walk. (Photograph by kind permission of Alison McCormack)

Deans Community High truly lives up to its title, because as well as providing education for over 800 teenage pupils, it also welcomes adult members of the community to join its daytime classes. Those pictured were taking part in a jewellery course working with silver and gold. The participants are, from left to right, Karen Hunter, Eric Forbes, Morag Forbes and Helen MacDonald. (Photograph by kind permission of Alison McCormack)

Adult student Jackie Stirling enjoys working in one of the art rooms at Deans Community High School where she studies drawing and painting. (Photograph by kind permission of Alison McCormack)

These adult students are hard at work in the art department. (Photograph by kind permission of Alison McCormack)

Over the years Deans Community High School has pioneered many modern educational methods, including flexible timetables for both pupils and staff, and was the first secondary school in West Lothian to give up the use of corporal punishment as a means of maintaining discipline. One of its most successful innovations has been paired reading in which older pupils encourage younger ones with their work. Here fifth former Liza Gilhooly is seen listening to second year pupil Mhairi Baird in another of the Livingston school's successful ideas, its comfortably furnished, attractive, brightly decorated Need to Read Room. (Photograph by kind permission of Alison McCormack)

Many trees have matured in the grounds of Deans Community High School, as seen in this picture of some of the school's first year pupils. (Photograph by kind permission of Alison McCormack)

Gathered in front of the entrance of Deans Community High, these first formers are about to set out on the school's annual sponsored walk. (Photograph by kind permission of Alison McCormack)

Senior pupils from Deans Community High School always take part in Livingston's annual twenty-four hour 'Relay for Life' event. Here nine of them are pictured with their mascot in front of their tents at Craigswood. (Photograph by kind permission of Alison McCormack)

Striking a pose in their attractively designed leotards are the members of Deans Community High School's 1999 prize-winning gymnastics team. The girls, who are trained by the school's sports coordinator, Moira Jackson, are from left to right, back row: Lisa McLaughlan, Laura McKenna, Heather Hunter, Lisa Burnside, Lisa Brown. Front row: Sheila Sharp, Linda Fowler. The girls were pictured in the school grounds by well-known school photographers Tempest.(Published by kind permission of Deans Community High.)

Livingston's Roman Catholic pupils originally had to travel to St Mary's Secondary School, Bathgate, for their secondary education, but are now served by the magnificent St Margaret's Academy. This ultra-modern building is designed on the principle of the American shopping mall high school, with each of its curriculum departments opening invitingly off a wide main street. Following its opening, St Mary's was closed and later demolished, and this fine new school now caters for Catholic pupils from approximately half of West Lothian, in tandem with St Kentigern's High School in Blackburn. In its wooded setting, St Margaret's also has equally impressive school grounds with a full range of sports facilities for the enjoyment of its 1,000 eleven to eighteen year old pupils, who take pride in wearing their school's smart maroon and grey uniform. (Picture by Dr Arthur Down)

From one of Livingston's newest schools to its oldest, historic Bellsquarry Primary, whose Victorian-style sandstone building is still in use. Its tall, narrow windows were designed to allow light into the classrooms without the distraction of its pupils being able to waste time by looking out. Today, however, under popular head teacher Linda Wood, its methods are as modern as any other school in Livingston. During the 1999 summer holidays its facilities were added to by the completion of a new modern teaching block situated in the former playground behind the original building, designed to cope with the expansion of roll, which at the Millennium had already increased to over one hundred and fifty.

A class from a past era at Bellsquarry Primary posed with their teacher for this class group photograph.

The current increase in roll at Bellsquarry is in marked contrast to thirty years ago when in 1970 five year-old Ian Piercy was the only Primary One pupil. Here young Ian's school outfit of shorts and casual polo shirt is in marked contrast to the school wear of the pupils in the previous photograph. Ian is seen in the playground of the village school on the first morning of the new term in August 1970, while other older pupils looked on with interest.

The entrance to Bellsquarry Primary still has a distinctly village feel to it despite its growing popularity with Livingston parents and its steady increase in roll.

These pupils are hard at work in their classroom at Letham Primary School, where Miss Rae Rutherford is the long-established and much respected head teacher. The following sequence of photographs taken at the school depicts the modern approach to primary education in Livingston.

Learning to listen carefully is an important starting point for these Primary One pupils who were among Letham's 1997 new entrants.

A year later, these two attractive youngsters piecing together this jigsaw puzzle were among the pupils in the school's new primary one class.

Making music is an important part of the well-balanced integrated curriculum taught at Letham Primary. Gone are the days when music lessons consisted simply of a whole class singing, as these enthusiastic youngsters experiment with percussion instruments and learn to appreciate rhythm.

Art too is well taught at Letham. Here pupils are seen putting the finishing touches to one of the giant lanterns which they made for the torchlight procession in which they participated at Howden Park in 1997.

Watch this space! Letham Primary is well equipped with computers and even the youngest pupils are very much at home with the latest technology before they cut their secondary teeth, as these Primary Three pupils happily showed in 1997.

Morning assembly is a regular event at Letham and this nativity play was presented at Christmas 1997.

Letham Primary also has a nursery school attached to it, which is much appreciated by local mothers.

Head teacher Miss Rae Rutherford is always keen to encourage her pupils to take a pride in their school, as demonstrated by this anti-litter project in 1996.

To protect the school's carpeted areas pupils take off their shoes as they come inside the school building.

On the other hand, when it comes to the ever popular morning playtime they get suitably clad for the Scottish weather.

Morning break is always time for having fun as these girls showed in 1997 when they took this upside-down view of the world.

Adding to the playground fun the following year in 1998 was this visit from Fyffes Bananas Van whose enthusiastic young staff encouraged the Letham pupils to take part in a Bananas in Pyjamas Party. Fyffes has established its large Scottish distribution warehouse on the northern edge of Livingston, thus becoming one of many firms to appreciate the new town's central position and excellent communication links to all parts of the country.

Seven
Livingston at Play

As a purpose built New Town , Livingston is very well provided with sports and leisure facilities, including an indoor swimming pool, a championship-standard eighteen hole golf course, an ultra-modern sports stadium and a ten pin bowling alley. Livingston residents are particularly proud of the town's football team, which plays at the sports stadium and whose successful progress into the Scottish First Division has put the town very much on the map. The team began its existence in Edinburgh as Meadowbank Thistle, but it is since the players moved out to Livingston that they have enjoyed far greater successes, encouraged by the support of the people of the New Town. As well as spectating at football matches, however, Livingston folk, both young and old, participate in a wide variety of sporting activities, some of which are depicted on the following pages.

Many Livingston boys and girls are enthusiastic members of local football clubs and turn out for regular weekly practices in the hope of one day playing at the neighbouring football stadium. (Photograph by kind permission of Dr Arthur Down)

Livingston Stadium, sponsored by the district's popular local newspaper the 'West Lothian Courier' is one of the most modern in Scotland, and the success of the local team has done much to put the town on the map. (Photograph by kind permission of Dr Arthur Down)

Livingston FC began life as Meadowbank Thistle, a third division side based at the famous Edinburgh stadium built for the Commonwealth Games, but whose performance never lived up to the impressive setting in which they played their home matches. Then came the decision to relocate to Livingston and with the change of venue came a change in fortunes, which has delighted their many New Town fans. Here Livingston Club Chairman Dominic Keane and Club Chief Executive, the colourful Jim Leishman, are seen in November 1998 revealing their exciting plans for the further development of the stadium, which is already one of the best grounds in Scotland. As well as being one of Scotland's most dynamic footballing personalities, Jim is also a poet and has even appeared as the dame in a professional pantomime. (Photograph by kind permission of the *West Lothian Courier*)

The effervescent Jim Leishman was in jubilant party mood in April 1996, when as manager he celebrated Livingston's success in becoming the Bell's Scottish Third Division Champions by beating Arbroath. The club's subsequent promotion into the Second Division was a move successfully achieved and aided by sponsorship from local electronic giants Mitsubishi. (Picture by kind permission of the *West Lothian Courier*)

Livingston skipper Jim Sherry (right) welcomed Manchester United captain Terry Looke at the official opening of Livingston Stadium at this floodlit match on 27 October 1998. (Photograph by kind permission of the *West Lothian Courier*, which carries full reports of all of Livingston FC's home and away fixtures.)

In 1999, Livingston climbed even further up the Scottish football league ladder when they won the Bell's Second Division Championship and promotion to the Scottish First Division. Here team manager Roy Stewart (left) celebrates winning the coveted league flag, with three of his senior players, David Bingham, Allan McManus and John Millar. (Photograph by kind permission of the *West Lothian Courier*)

Livingston striker Gerry Britton gets the better of Rangers defender Scott Wilson. (Photograph by kind permission of the *West Lothian Courier*)

Letham Primary School pupils love their football as the start of every morning playtime proves – they never waste a moment getting onto the ball!

The boys and girls of Letham are also encouraged to take an interest in a wide range of sporting activities, as this 1971 school sports day picture shows. Unfortunately, the disappointingly dull weather on this June summer day made it as hard to spot the sun as to spot the ball when these pupils tried their hands at the netball shoot.

Livingston is also justifiably proud of Bubbles, its indoor swimming complex with its modern fun pool and associated attractions.

Livingston was the first place in Scotland to offer its youngsters the challenge and excitement of a purpose-built skate boarding ramp.

The well-laid out jogging course and trim trail in the sheltered valley of the River Almond is also a popular keep-fit attraction in the heart of Livingston. The course was designed and laid out in 1978.

Each of the stations on the trim trail offers a different challenge to its enthusiastic young users.

Negotiating the logs is the first obstacle on the course.

A close-up view of the second obstacle, also seen in the background of the previous photograph.

The third station on the trim trail offers a steep clamber over this timber pyramid.

Another of the stations on the trim trail.

Strong arms are needed for this final challenge.

Livingston Development Corporation employed artists to create features in many areas of the New Town including this futuristic effort, which these local children nicknamed 'The Wiggle.'

Best known of the Livingston sculptures is this one entitled 'Community', which graces the town centre at Almondvale and seems to excellently sum up the enthusiasm and energy of this enterprising new town.

Livingston Development Corporation was equally eager to preserve the history of the area and preserved Barracks Farm as a community centre.

Eight
Almond Valley
Heritage Centre

Livingston Development Corporation gave every encouragement when several of its employees led by Bill Turnbull, Forsyth Jamieson and Alastair Weir, following their attendance at a University of Edinburgh Extra Mural Course on the history of the area, decided to bring back to life one aspect of the New Town's past, a disused water mill on the north bank of the River Almond, near their offices in the LDC's original headquarters. The enthusiastic local historians found out that the mill belonged to Lord Primrose, now the Earl of Rosebery, and sought a meeting with him to put forward their proposals. In October 1970 his Lordship met them on site and gave his enthusiastic backing to their ambitious restoration scheme, promising to help them with materials from his estate at Temple in Mid Lothian. With this support behind them, the Livingston Mill Restoration group was officially founded in December 1970 and for over four years its enthusiastic members put in thousands of unpaid back-breaking hours of work every weekend and on countless evenings digging out the long lade, which brought water from the River Almond to power the old mill wheel, sawing new timbers and shoring up the crumbling masonry. The whole building was then re-roofed. The help of staff and students at West Lothian College of Further Education was sought to assist with the more technical aspects of the reconstruction, while offers of assistance with labouring and other manual chores from pupils from local high schools and students from Moray House College of Education in Edinburgh were warmly welcomed. Finally, on Saturday 26 April 1975, Lord Rosebery was invited back to set the mill wheel in motion again for the first time.

This success led the members of the Restoration Group to decide that if the mill was to be ensured a proper setting, and be seen in its proper context, then it was essential that the adjacent farm and its traditional Scottish steading with its many varied outbuildings should be preserved as well. The farm had been tenanted for almost two hundred years by the well-known Buchanan family, but as the New Town progressively encroached upon more and more of its fields, they had recently moved out. The way was therefore clear for the creation of the Livingston Mill Community Farm Project and Forsyth Jamieson was appointed as the new Farm Manager. Since then the whole complex has developed even further, with the creation of the Almond Valley Heritage Centre, incorporating the Scottish Shale-Oil Museum. Under its Curator, Dr Robin Chesters, Administrator Elaine Dunsire, Visitor Services Officer Carol McDonald and Farm Officer Carol Johnston, the centre is already one of the largest and most successful visitor centres in Scotland. On the eve of the Millennium it was announced that it had received funding of half a million pounds to improve its museum and transform it into an exciting new hands-on learning and discovering experience.

The pantiled roof of the historic mill building is seen in the background against the trees in the valley of the Almond whose waters power the big mill wheel. (Picture by John Doherty)

The interior of the old mill which was restored to working order by the enthusiasts of the Livingston Mill Restoration Group. (Picture by John Doherty)

The old mill required lots of work from the restoration enthusiasts and while work progressed the massive wooden wheel was protected by this shelter. When first brought back to working order it was capable of powering one pair of massive grinding stones, a bruiser and some of the ancillary machinery, but since then its capacity has been increased to drive an even wider range of equipment. (Picture by John Doherty)

One of the large millstones is seen here outside the farm dairy, whose equipment was also powered by the adjacent water mill. (Picture by John Doherty)

The restoration project at Livingston's historic Mill Farm proved so successful and so popular that it has now developed into the Almond Valley Heritage Centre. The red pantiled roofed buildings of the farm steading are seen in this picture along with one of the old farm carts. Tractor and trailer rides around the farm to see the crops growing in the fields along the banks of the River Almond are also a popular attraction.

Livingston New Town's young residents love to come to Almond Valley Heritage Centre to feed the many pet animals at Mill Farm, including these two affectionate goats. Ducks, geese, hens and chickens now bring lots of life to the old farm steading and in the spring there are always lambs and calves for the children to feed. In what is described as 'the uninvited guests area' there is also the opportunity to observe the secret residents of the farm as rats, mice and beetles scurry around!

Almond Valley's most popular resident, Big Ben the Clydesdale Horse. Throughout the year many special events are held at Almond Valley Heritage Centre. These include a harvest weekend at the beginning of September when old farm equipment is dusted down and employed to bring in the crops and visitors are invited to try their hands at stacking wheat sheaves and even 'tattie haukin'. Easter, Halloween and Christmas are all celebrated in traditional Scottish fashion with hard boiled eggs to roll, turnip lanterns to be carved out and Santa Claus to bid welcome.

One of the original enthusiasts who began the whole Livingston Mill project, Forsyth Jamieson harnesses Big Ben to take visitors on cart rides. The farm site also features a well laid out nature trail, a picnic area and an adventure area for children.

Mr Jamieson is equally enthusiastic about the narrow gauge railway whose track has been created as an added attraction for the many visitors to Almond Valley Heritage Centre, and to transport them around its large attractive twenty acre site. He is seen here chatting to another of the Heritage Centre's staff, Alex Ogg. A special Railway Shunt Weekend is held every August. At present the railway track runs as far as the Mill Weir on the River Almond and there are plans to extend it further in the future and to feature more of the type of locomotives and rolling stock associated with the Scottish mineral oil industry. The centre already possesses several drum shaped oil wagons and some of the bogies which carried the shale from the mines to the retorts. The centre is open all year and train, tractor and trailer rides are available every weekend from Easter to October and every day during July and August.

The Almond Valley Heritage Centre was honoured by a royal visit from Her Majesty Queen Elizabeth and the Duke of Edinburgh on 30 June 1987.

Her Majesty unveiled a plaque to record her visit, and it can be seen on the stone walls of the old farm steading.

The royal visit to Almond Valley Heritage Centre.

Before leaving the farm, Her Majesty was presented with a bouquet by that year's Livingston Station Gala Queen, who had herself been crowned on the first Saturday of the month.